The Couple's Strategy for Building Wealth

Rick,

So glad you bought the book! Hopefully, it will be a good investment (but not that you need it!).

Enjoy!

Laura Bell

The Couple's Strategy for Building Wealth

Myths, Mindsets and Money

Laura Bell

Copyright © 2016 by Laura Bell

Mill City Press, Inc.
322 First Avenue N, 5th floor
Minneapolis, MN 55401
612.455.2293
www.millcitypublishing.com

All rights reserved. No part of this publication may be reproduced,
stored in a retrieval system, or transmitted, in any form or by
any means, electronic, mechanical, photocopying, recording, or
otherwise, without the prior written permission of the author.

ISBN-13: 978-1-63413-878-9
LCCN: 2016901213

Cover Design by Oliver Wieckowski and Alan Pranke

Printed in the United States of America

*To couples committed to
building a wealthy future together.*

CONTENTS

Preface ix

Introduction xiii

PART 1
The Spending Mindset

Chapter 1	Spending Mindset #1: Lack of Alignment on the Financial Future	3
Chapter 2	Spending Mindset #2: My Money vs. Your Money	7
Chapter 3	Spending Mindset #3: Wants = Needs	11
Chapter 4	Spending Mindset #4: We Buy What We Can Afford and Spend What We Make	17
Chapter 5	Spending Mindset #5: Saving = Feeling Restricted and Deprived of "Things"	21
Chapter 6	Spending Mindset #6: Saving = Spending Less on the Same Stuff	25
Chapter 7	A Summary of the Spending Mindset	29

PART 2
The Wealth Mindset

Chapter 8	Wealth Mindset #1: Deep Alignment on Financial Planning for the Future	35
Chapter 9	Wealth Mindset #2: Our Money, Our Future	41

Chapter 10	Wealth Mindset #3: We Buy What We Need	47
Chapter 11	Wealth Mindset #4: Savings = Abundance and Freedom	53
Chapter 12	Wealth Mindset #5: Saving = Not Spending	59
Chapter 13	A Summary of the Wealth Mindset	63

PART 3
The Spend One, Save One Couple's Strategy for Wealth: Bringing It All Together

Chapter 14	The Spend One, Save One Couple's Strategy for Wealth	69
Chapter 15	Simplifying Your Money Management	73
Chapter 16	Simplifying Your Money Management: Finding Synergies	79
Chapter 17	Implement Your Spend One, Save One Couple's Strategy for Wealth	93
Chapter 18	What If the Spend One, Save One Couple's Strategy for Wealth Can't Work for You?	97

Conclusion   101
About the Author   103

Preface

This book represents one of the biggest contributions I feel I can make to couples who are building a life together. If you read it and embrace it fully, it will allow you and your partner to save more money than you ever thought possible. How do I know this? This book outlines how my husband and I saved a lot of money over the years, certainly more than I ever thought we could. Today, we are living the life of our dreams because of the strategies described in this book.

During the spring of 1994, my husband Erwin and I had recently settled into our new apartment. We had both completed our university educations and were in the early stages of our careers. One sunny Saturday afternoon, probably over a glass of wine, we came up with a simple strategy for building our wealth together as a couple. Even though it was a very simple concept, this strategy dramatically altered our mindset around saving and spending money *forever*. Equally important, it also created a wonderful foundation for us to start thinking and living as a couple. That was over twenty years ago. We implemented this strategy—the "Spend One, Save One Couple's Strategy for Wealth"—that very day, and we've been living by that same strategy ever since. The wealthy lifestyle we enjoy today is due in large part to implementing that strategy and sticking to it.

While I've shared a little about our approach to saving with friends and family over the years, it had become such an unconscious, habitual way of living for us that I really didn't give it too much thought—until I met a young colleague on a consulting engagement during the fall of 2011. He had recently moved in with his fiancée and they were starting to plan their future together. His situation was reminiscent of Erwin and me starting out years earlier, and so I thought he might be interested in an approach to saving that had worked really well for us. We had more than one conversation on this topic, and each time my colleague became more and more interested, realizing the difference it could make in his life and in his future with his fiancée. They started implementing the strategy and saw some incredible results in a very short period of time that altered their future dramatically. It was a challenge at first, but they persevered until their saving habits become habitual and natural. In watching their success, it became clear to me that the concepts in this book that I thought were "obvious" or "basic" were in fact much more than that—they were transformational and could have a potentially profound impact on a couple's financial future. My colleague's success, coupled with my own experience, inspired me to share my strategy with other couples in this book.

What This Book Is

This book represents an opportunity for working couples who are committed to building a life together to think differently about spending and saving. It presents a simple, yet powerful approach to building wealth as a couple. There is a level of discipline and commitment that must be in place in order to succeed with this strategy. You will get out of this approach what you put into it. It is something that you and your partner can implement, should you so choose, for a month, a year, ten years, or the rest of your lives. Your level of success and how much money you save will be directly correlated to your level of commitment. As you read this book, you can "try on" the ideas presented here much as you would a new suit. If you don't like how it feels, you put the idea back on the rack. Even if you don't implement the strategy, you will at least learn something, think differently about saving, and pick up a few good habits along the way.

What This Book Is *Not*

This book does *not* lay out a risky get-rich-quick scheme. This is *not* a guide about investing. There are plenty of great books on investing out there already. Rather, it is a safe and reliable "get-rich-slow" scheme. The Spend One, Save One Couple's Strategy for Wealth is a long-term strategy for committed couples looking to build financial freedom and wealth. This book is about saving money—how you invest and grow your wealth beyond this strategy is up to you. This book will get you to the starting line, where you will have enough liquid cash to become a serious investor if you choose to do so.

Introduction

- *Why Financial Planning Books Aren't Working*
- *How Saving Money Is Like Losing Weight*
- *Getting Your Mind over Your Money*

Why Financial Planning Books Aren't Working

We have a big, big problem in the United States. People are not saving enough money, and as a result, they live life fearing how they'll afford retirement and unforeseen financial crises. While it is true that since the financial crisis of 2008, many families have reduced their debt, the overwhelming majority of couples still has depleted savings and has done little or nothing to save for retirement. I've seen statistics and read articles that suggested as much as 40 percent of working Americans are not saving for retirement and 25 percent of American families have no savings at all. How could it possibly be that so many couples and households find themselves in this financial situation when hundreds of books have been written on the topics of financial planning and investing? Part of the problem lies in the fact that the traditional pathways to wealth are shrinking. For instance:

- Consistently double-digit annualized returns in the stock market are no longer a sure thing.

- Steady home appreciation is no longer certain and home prices are more volatile now than in the past.
- Stable job markets and reliable career advancement are rarer, and good jobs for new college graduates are harder to find than ever before.
- Consistent base salary increases are becoming more intermittent in spite of an improving job market.

As a result, people don't have money to invest in the first place anymore—and even the best books about investing are worthless unless you have the money to invest. Perhaps the only sure way to *guarantee* a prosperous future and comfortable retirement in today's volatile markets is to *save* more money than ever before. More specifically, people need to stop spending most or all of the money they make.

How Saving Money Is Like Losing Weight

Telling people to stop spending all of the money they make and save it instead is like telling them to eat less junk food and more fruits and vegetables to lose weight. The concept might be easy to get, but translating the concept into action is a whole different story. It's much easier said than done. And for most couples, saving money is like losing weight—they might "know" what to do but falter miserably in the execution. That's because knowing how to do something does not guarantee action. People might "know" that to lose weight you exercise more and consume fewer calories. You stop eating junk food and replace it with fruits and vegetables. There are hundreds of books detailing many different effective strategies for losing

Introduction

weight. So why do so many people struggle to lose weight? Why don't people take action? Similarly, people might "know" how to save money—making automatic transfers to savings accounts, cutting up credit cards, preparing and sticking to a budget, etc.—and there are dozens of books detailing many different effective strategies for saving money. Yet people don't do it. So why do so many people struggle to save money? Why don't people take action? It's because knowing how to do something does not guarantee taking action. Many people struggle to lose weight because there are thoughts, desires, and motivations at play in the background that are overriding the commitment to lose weight. Similarly, many people struggle to save money because there are thoughts, desires, and motivations at play in the background that are overriding the commitment to stop spending and save more. Knowing about effective strategies to save money (which can be easily learned through books and websites) does not always translate into action.

No matter what people "know," their actions are always consistent with their underlying thoughts, desires, and motivations. For example, just because someone knows that losing weight will require eliminating processed sugar from their diet does not guarantee they won't enjoy the Christmas goodies brought in by their work colleagues. If there is an underlying thought that says, "It won't hurt your diet just to have a little. Go ahead; you deserve it and these goodies are only available once a year," then the goody will most likely be eaten. A person's underlying thinking or motivations usually trump knowledge. That is why understanding and uncovering underlying thought patterns is critical to changing actions and ultimately results. Books that focus on "actions" and telling people what to do often fall short because they don't address the thinking in the background that is ultimately driving behaviors. For people struggling to save money, the first and most challenging thing to address is the underlying thoughts that are preventing saving and encouraging spending. The knowledge of how to save is much easier to put into action when your thinking is consistent with saving money.

Getting Your Mind over Your Money

For couples to save more money, they first need to understand what the often invisible and undetectable thought patterns are that are contributing to their inability to meet their savings goals. A dramatic shift in how couples *think* about saving money is required to drive new saving behaviors.

Part I of this book will explore six Spending Mindsets to help couples become more aware of the kind of thinking that encourages an undisciplined and habitual approach to spending. These consistent and persistent thoughts become entrenched and accepted as "truths" over time rather than as mindsets or beliefs that can be changed. You can't change a mindset until you see it as one possible way to think rather than the *only* way to think. These paradigms or beliefs about money and spending are not necessarily bad ways to think, but there are other paradigms exemplified in "The Wealth Mindset" (Part 2) that are more consistent with saving money.

Part 2 of this book will explore five Wealth Mindsets that enable couples to migrate from living in a Spending Mindset to living in a Wealth Mindset. Thinking about saving money in new ways is the precursor to acting in new ways; for many couples, only changes in behavior can bring new results and increased prosperity.

Part 3 of this book explores the Spend One, Save One Couple's Strategy for Wealth, which provides couples with a specific, step-by-step, proven roadmap to put a Wealth Mindset into practice and force the adoption of new behaviors. Ultimately, the couples that can master and control their mindsets will gain control of their financial future.

PART 1

The Spending Mindset

CHAPTER 1

Spending Mindset #1: Lack of Alignment on the Financial Future

- *Money: The "Avoided" Conversation*
- *What If You Can't Agree on Household Spending?*
- *Feeling Lucky? Living Life without a Savings Plan*
- *Key Takeaways*

Money: The "Avoided" Conversation

We've all heard it: Sex, money, and kids are among the top topics that cause couples to fight and, in some cases, to divorce. There's no doubt that money is an emotional topic for many people. Everything from what people earn to what and who they spend it on is wrapped up in personal self-worth, values, and beliefs. How people relate to money and savings is also very personal and unique. This might explain why many couples avoid talking about money and the spending patterns in their households. It is a difficult topic that requires a lot of patience, understanding, and negotiation. The money conversation can be an emotional quagmire, fraught with landmines at every turn, and to speak openly as a couple about it can require a degree of savvy communication skills that most people simply do not have. I know of a woman who manages the finances in her house; at one point, she was two months behind on the mortgage and her husband didn't even know it! Now there's a fight waiting to happen. It has me wondering how many people are not only avoiding talking about their finances but are actually keeping secrets from their spouse about spending "improprieties" and secret debt. I'm not one of those people who believes your spouse has to know *everything* about you (past romantic relationships would be a good example of things better left private, in my opinion), but finances and how household earnings are spent are not topics to be kept secret.

What If You Can't Agree on Household Spending?

When couples avoid the deep, meaningful conversations that will guide their saving and spending habits throughout a marriage, there is a lack of alignment, few agreed-upon goals, little or no vision for the future, and the potential for huge battles over money throughout the marriage. Couples living in a Spending Mindset tend to avoid these conversations. Many couples have discussed a short-term budget and have some general rules, but that isn't the same as having an agreed-upon savings plan that will guide saving and spending habits for years to come. Without a long-term plan, couples live and spend more in the moment, looking only at daily and weekly needs, and can often end up fighting about what the priorities really are. Without frequent discussions around money and the creation of a solid, long-term savings plan, priorities can often become misaligned and couples are more likely to fight and bicker. The opposite is also true: Couples who align around a savings plan and have mutual agreement around spending and savings priorities will fight less about money and are more likely to build a prosperous future. This is a classic case of a "pay now or pay later" scenario: Either have the difficult conversations with your spouse today and negotiate until you can come to agreement or risk more significant and emotionally painful battles later when a financial crisis hits or significant financial decisions have to be made. So, where do you fit on the spectrum? How comfortable are you talking with your spouse about money?

It can be very difficult for newly married couples in their twenties or even thirties to plan for life in their sixties. It seems so very far away and it looks like it will be forever before you retire. There is also a lot of temptation to buy things *now*. Couples that are just starting out have long lists of things they want to buy. Having said that, starting a foundation for financial prosperity early on is hugely advantageous. A short- and long-term savings plan that the couple is aligned around governs buying decisions and dictates how much money will be saved. Without a plan, buying decisions are governed by everything else—desires, whims, disposable cash, sales, and impulses, all of which are rarely shared by both partners equally. That's where the fighting can start. When you are aligned around short- and long-term savings plans, buying decisions are governed only by those plans, which eliminate disagreements and unnecessary spending.

Feeling Lucky? Living Life without a Savings Plan

Without a long-term savings plan, security and financial independence happen only by chance rather than by design.

out plans tend to have more troubles weathering storms (like the meltdown of 2008). Granted, it is very ..cult to plan for a rainy day when the sun is shining, but the rain will come, and, God willing, you will someday be a couple in your sixties looking retirement in the face. Will that face be smiling at you or telling you to go back to work for another ten years because you can't afford to retire yet? Building a life together without a savings plan you are aligned around is like betting on the lottery. You might have great success without a plan, but the odds will be stacked against you.

Key Takeaways

- Couples living in a Spending Mindset tend to avoid deep, meaningful conversations about money and are therefore not aligned around their financial future.
- A lack of alignment around household savings and spending goals leaves future prosperity to chance.
- Alignment around household savings and spending offers couples a critical foundation for not only financial success but marital success and happiness as well.

CHAPTER 2

Spending Mindset #2: My Money vs. Your Money

- *Why Some Couples Keep Their Finances Separate*
- *The Pitfalls of Keeping Finances Separate*
- *The Case for Joining Finances*
- *Key Takeaways*

Why Some Couples Keep Their Finances Separate

The key characteristic of Spending Mindset #2 is the propensity to keep earnings and spending habits separate and distinct in the marriage. Pretty much everything has been amalgamated in the marriage (home, last name, furniture, etc.) *except* the money. This is especially true if the couple hasn't aligned around short- and long-term financial goals for the household (see Chapter 1) and each spouse is exercising their individual spending habits and patterns. While these couples might have one or two joint accounts, each one keeps separate bank accounts and tends to have separate financial responsibilities in the household. For example, one partner pays the mortgage, the other pays the childcare provider, and each pays for their own car loan, etc.

This financial strategy is not all bad. First of all, it's fair. The couple shares expenses, typically in a ratio relative to each spouse's income; for example, if one partner makes significantly more money than the other, then he or she will take on a bigger share of the expenses. This strategy also allows each person to feel they are controlling their income and are able to exercise freedom in how they spend their hard-earned income after they pay their share of the expenses. Third, this strategy clarifies each person's financial obligation in the marriage and therefore ensures that expenses get paid. Fourth, the strategy is pretty easy to execute: The couple divides up the expenses in an equitable manner and then each is on their own to manage their piece of the pie, so to speak. Finally, this is a "comfortable" budgeting approach for those couples that don't really "trust" their partner with regard to money; they feel far better knowing at least some, if not all of their own paycheck is going into a bank account only they can access.

The Pitfalls of Keeping Finances Separate

While this household money management approach is rational and can work very well, it can also have some dire consequences for building wealth. First, what tends to happen is that couples spend what they have left over after meeting their financial liabilities in the marriage rather than putting it into a shared pot of savings. Or, at the very minimum, the money left over is viewed as "personal" money that will be spent or saved at the discretion of the *individual*, rather than the couple. This is especially true if the couple has not created and aligned around a long-term savings plan. So rather than looking at that "leftover" money as a pathway for building wealth for the household, it is seen as discretionary money to be used as each spouse sees fit as an individual. More often than not, that means much of the money will be spent. The second consequence is that two individuals operating their finances as individuals cannot take advantage of the financial synergies that are available when couples share credit cards, saving accounts, and, most important, an overall strategy for how money will be spent. Operating one bank account with a higher balance might eliminate fees and pay a higher interest rate as compared to two lower-balance bank accounts that pay less interest and charge more fees. (More such synergies will be explored in Part 3.) Finally, if one spouse earns significantly more than the other, this can cause some stress in the relationship. I know a couple that has always kept their finances completely separate, including their incomes, savings, 401K plans, and nonregistered investments. One partner has far more money than the other, so if they want to have a really nice vacation, the husband typically has to "treat" his wife since she can't really afford it. I hear that and I think "yuck." That just doesn't sound right to me at all and sounds like a pitfall to happiness.

The Case for Joining Finances

While this topic will be explored in more depth in Chapter 9, a case can be built for joining finances (which means all income is pooled and all accounts are joint accounts). As already mentioned, couples can take better advantage of financial synergies when they are a single financial entity. Joining finances also makes it easier to fulfill a joint long-term savings plan. It's difficult to fulfill a joint plan when you're operating financially independently at the same time. There is also a distinct psychological impact on the marriage when the money is pooled. I remember going to Las Vegas with my sister-in-law frequently before I had children. We would always pool our gambling money before we hit the blackjack tables. We set some guidelines and the budget and then had fun. Because we pooled our money, we never had a "loser" or "winner." The *team* was either up or down, and it always seemed to happen that if one of us was down on our luck, the other would be doing well. It created a team feeling and eliminated jealousy or upset. Pooling finances in a marriage can have the same psychological benefit. You become a team, aligned around your financial goals. It creates a real sense of togetherness. Finally, at the end of the day, managing fewer financial accounts and credit cards is easier and takes less time. Life is busy enough and accounts and credit cards have to be watched very carefully today for unusual activity. Having both individuals in a marriage managing numerous duplicate accounts doesn't make much sense.

Key Takeaways

- Couples living in a Spending Mindset tend to keep their earnings and spending habits separate and while that can be a good strategy in some ways, it can have negative consequences for building wealth.
- When couples keep their finances separate, "leftover" money tends to be spent rather than saved.
- Joining finances allows for synergies, fulfillment of long-term savings plans, and a potentially more harmonious relationship.

CHAPTER 3
Spending Mindset # 3: Wants = Needs

- *Wants Often Masquerade as Needs*
- *When Wants and Needs Are Confused in Our Minds*
- *Exercise: Are You Spending on Needs or Wants?*
- *Key Takeaways*

Wants Often Masquerade as Needs

If you ask people to stop and think about how a want is different from a need, they will probably be able to clearly distinguish one from the other. As concepts, people get that these two things are clearly different. The problem is that when people are living in a Spending Mindset day in and day out, they are not really conscious of this difference when it comes to making buying decisions. The line between wants and needs is blurred and, over time, everything that's interesting or desirable around them looks like something they *need* to buy.

In all fairness, wants and needs are fairly close by definition:

Need: *Verb* To require (something) because it is essential or very important; "I need help now"; an urgent *want*.

Need: *Noun* Circumstances in which something is necessary, or that require some course of action; necessity: "the need for food."

Want: *Verb* To have a desire to possess or do (something); wish for; to feel the *need* or desire for.

Want: *Noun* A lack or deficiency of something.

Perhaps it's not surprising that these two concepts become confused in our minds, especially given the fact that both terms appear in the definition of the other. Recently, I heard a friend say, "I need a new pair of shoes." I said to myself (looking at the nice-looking pair of shoes already on her feet and thinking about the twenty or so pairs I've seen in her walk-in closet, "Do you really *need* a new pair of shoes, or do you just *want* a new pair of shoes?" It is obvious to me that her "desire to possess" a new pair of shoes is a want, and it was equally obvious to me that in her mind, it was a need that *had* to be satisfied. This is a perfect example of a want masquerading as a need—one of the true enemies of saving money. What about the "need" for a bigger house? One of the things I hear couples say a lot is that they "need a bigger house" or they "need to upgrade the kitchen". This isn't really a need at all (assuming safe shelter is available); rather, it is a want. Not buying a bigger house or upgrading their kitchen would leave them feeling unsatisfied at worst. If you have children or have ever spent time with them, you might notice they think and talk like everything is a need. Even when they say they "want" something, they act like it's much more of a need and they'll die if they don't get it. We grow out of this as we mature but even as adults, this mindset can prevail. For many couples, there is very little distinction between wants and needs when it comes to shopping. For certain purchases (clothes, new cars, restaurant dining), they think and talk as if many things are needs and they just simply have to have them.

When Wants and Needs Are Confused in Our Minds

Relating to wants as needs causes a lot of unnecessary and automatic spending that could be avoided. We are compelled to satisfy what we view as our needs and can rationalize spending money on things we need much more easily than if we see those things as wants. We actually trick ourselves into believing our spending has more urgency than it really does. This doesn't mean that we shouldn't ever spend on wants, but we should do so consciously and responsibly. Consciously deciding to spend money on a want is quite different from unconsciously spending money on something that we've tricked ourselves into believing is a need. For example, if you're a gourmet cook and you and your spouse would really enjoy a remodeled kitchen, and if you recognize this as a "nice to have" rather than a "need to have," and, most of all, if it won't put your financial objectives at risk, then go for it! However, it should be clear to the couple that upgrading the kitchen is not a need. Unfortunately, most couples in a Spending Mindset are less likely to correctly distinguish between wants and needs; and if everything around you is a need, you end up spending much more money than you should. This of course is especially problematic when it puts your short-term or long-term financial goals at risk. Being able to distinguish needs from wants is a critical skill for wealth building. It allows for more discriminating spending. It's not wrong to want a bigger house or to buy another pair of shoes, but for couples to get out of this Spending Mindset, there has to be a realization that many of the things that look like needs are actually wants masquerading as needs—and not all wants should be satisfied. When a couple is able to see wants as different from needs, spending decisions can be infused with more thoughtfulness. As a result, unnecessary spending will be reduced. Spending less contributes to increased savings and increased savings build wealth. While this is all easy to understand, putting it into practice is difficult.

Exercise: Are You Spending on Needs or Wants?

When it comes to spending money, the best way to distinguish between a need and a want is to look at what will happen if the purchase is not made. Would it cause real harm or significant risk (a need)? Would it leave feelings of dissatisfaction and/or unhappiness (a want)? The purchase of baby formula for your baby is a need, as certain harm would come to your baby if her need for food is not met. Not buying a designer handbag is not going to cause real harm or significant risk (although I imagine some might argue with me on that one!). Use this definition as a guide as you complete the following exercise. You need to be very careful here in the way you total your wants vs. your needs. For example, say your grocery bill is $58.00. How much of that is need vs. want spending? The fresh produce, meat, and milk could be considered needs. The donuts, chocolate bars, and apple pie should be considered wants. You might have to really scrutinize each purchase to figure out how much is want spending and how much is need spending.

Spending Mindset # 3: Wants = Needs

Exercise

- Map out *all* spending over a two-week period (review credit card bills and other expenditure receipts).
- Indicate which items were needs and which were wants.
- How much money did you spend on needs?
- How much money did you spend on wants?
- Which purchases were wants masquerading as needs?
- Hang onto your table; you will need it again in Chapter 10, which will lay out a course to practice separating needs from wants.

Example

Needs vs. Wants Spending					
Purchase Item	$ Amount	Need	Want	Total $ Spent on Needs	Total $ Spent on Wants
Groceries	$58.00	√	√	$35.00	$23.00
Latte	$4.20		√		$4.20
Oil Change	$38.00	√		$38.00	
Dress Shoes	$84.00		√		$84.00
Etc.					
				NEEDS	WANTS
GRAND TOTALS				$73.00	$111.20
Percentage of Total Spend				40%	60%

In this simple example, you can see that of the couple's total spend, significantly more money has been spent on wants vs. needs. You might be quite surprised to see just how much of your money is being spent in similar proportions.

Key Takeaways

- When we are in a Spending Mindset, almost everything we spend money on looks like something we need—and we are more compelled to spend money on things we feel we need.
- When we can distinguish and separate our wants from our needs, we can choose to spend money on needs and save the money we would have spent on wants.
- It's OK to spend on wants as long as it's done consciously and doesn't put your savings goals at risk.

CHAPTER 4

Spending Mindset #4: We Buy What We Can Afford and Spend What We Make

- *The Amount We Can Afford Is the Starting Point for Most Purchasing Decisions*
- *Make More, Spend More*
- *Key Takeaways*

The Amount We Can Afford Is the Starting Point for Most Purchasing Decisions

The key characteristic of Spending Mindset #4 is the automatic tendency for couples to put their spending "ceiling" at the amount of money they have, plus the amount of debt they have at their disposal. In other words, the starting point for a lot of their purchasing decisions is the uppermost limit of how much they have to spend. For example, when couples are looking at buying a house, they often look at how much house they can *afford*. The first thing they do is go to a banker and ask "how big of a mortgage can I get?" Then they tell their real estate agent how big a mortgage they can get so the real estate agent looks for the most expensive house that syncs up with the biggest possible mortgage. Rather than shopping with a clear idea of what they need, they end up shopping at the ceiling of affordability. In a Spending Mindset, this is how couples shop—and the world at large expects people to shop this way, too.

Another example: My husband Erwin recently went shopping for a bathtub. The salesperson approached him and asked him how much he had to spend. The salesperson wanted to sell Erwin the most expensive bathtub he could. Erwin answered that he didn't want to talk in terms of how much he had to spend but rather the features and benefits that he needed and what the salesperson could offer based on that. The salesperson was somewhat surprised because most people are automatically wired to first offer how much money they have to spend (aka "afford") and then see what features and benefits they can get for that amount of money. As it turns out, one of the least expensive tubs was a perfect match for what Erwin needed. So while Erwin had $1,000 to spend, he got the tub he needed for $500.00 and saved $500.00 on the purchase. That savings delighted him. We consider that a huge win; namely, employing the type of thinking that encourages buying what is needed rather than what can be afforded. Ask yourself: Do you go into a store thinking about the features and benefits you require, or do you go into a store thinking about how much you have to spend? Most people tend to base their buying decisions on how much money they have to spend, and salespeople are very tuned into this (especially those paid on commission). I'm not suggesting that it's a bad idea to know the maximum amount you can spend on something. Quite the contrary—you should always know your spending ceiling before you shop for anything. What I am suggesting is that the maximum amount you have to spend shouldn't be the starting point for your purchasing decisions. In a spending mindset, people are automatically programmed to spend all they can afford to spend. Couples are often unconscious of the fact that they don't *have* to spend up to their ceiling. This often unquestioned approach to buying causes people to spend a lot more money than necessary and saving a lot less than they could. When Erwin and I went shopping for a new house in Charlotte, North Carolina, we did two things: 1) We set a spending ceiling based on a comfortable cash flow for us that fit our short- and long-term savings goals; and 2) we determined what size of home we needed. Our purchasing decision had nothing to do with how much we could afford. In fact, none of our purchasing decisions start off with how much we *can* spend. Start noticing how salespeople, advertisers, and the people around you are geared to encourage you to spend as much as possible. Are you taking the bait? Ask yourselves what happens when you have "excess" money left over after you have paid all of your expenses. Do you look and see what you can buy because you can "afford" it? Or do you save it? The marketplace doesn't want you to save it. It wants you to spend all that you have.

Make More, Spend More

Not only do couples tend to spend at the ceiling limit of their affordability, but their ceiling tends to go up as their income goes up. If, for instance, a couple's salary goes up $1.00, their spending ceiling goes up $1.00 as well; therefore, increases in income get spent rather than saved. This tends to be a pervasive habit for couples living in a Spending Mindset. It's the thinking that says as you make more money, you have to spend at a level proportional to the increase in income. As people make more money, they get fancier cars, bigger homes, and more expensive "toys." Spending at the uppermost limit is an unquestioned habit for many people. This behavior feels like a reward while in reality it's just unnecessary for the most part. Many couples do not need to spend all the money they make to have a wonderful, satisfying lifestyle; yet this mindset of buying what can be afforded goes unquestioned. People get a raise and automatically start thinking about what they can spend it on. In fact, many couples spend more than what they make and often carry high-interest balances on their credit cards. Ironically, in the United States, some of the highest earners in the country are also the poorest. They are the poorest because their debt levels are astronomical and therefore their monthly income goes to pay their debts. Couples don't need to spend all the money they make. Bonus checks do not need to be spent on more expensive things; in fact, bonus checks don't need to be spent at all in many cases.

Key Takeaways

- In a Spending Mindset, couples spend at the uppermost ceiling of what they can afford and tend to spend all the money they make, including increases in income and bonuses.
- The world is designed to encourage couples to spend as much money as they have—and beyond (by taking on more debt).
- Many couples could have a fantastic lifestyle spending less than what they make and could afford to spend.

CHAPTER 5

Spending Mindset #5: Saving = Feeling Restricted and Deprived of "Things"

- *But We Want It Now!*
- *Saving Money Isn't as Fun as Buying New Things*
- *Key Takeaways*

But We Want It Now!

The key characteristic of Spending Mindset #5 is the tendency to see saving money as a form of self-sacrifice and deprivation and spending money as a form of gratification—a "treat" or a reward for something. For example, "I've worked hard this week, so I'm going to treat myself to a new sweater or a nice dinner out this weekend." It's not too surprising that people feel that way given our society's tendency to want immediate gratification. People are automatically programmed to satisfy their desires now (because you *deserve* it, don't you?), not later and certainly not forty years from today, which is when the best savings plans start bearing fruit. People do not like the idea of "can't" have now but *can* have later. For many people, just hearing the word *can't* causes resistance. The mind begins to focus on what it can't have and gets stuck there until it gets its way. As a result, saving money rather than spending it on treats that make you feel good is an undesirable activity that gets a lot of resistance. It has the look and feel of deprivation, and nobody likes to feel deprived.

Saving Money Isn't as Fun as Buying New Things

In a Spending Mindset, not only does saving get associated with deprivation and self-sacrifice, but it doesn't look like much fun either. Spending money often provides joy and satisfaction. Saving money is boring and unsatisfying. Saving money is never as much fun as spending it. Picture yourself in a store looking at something you've wanted to buy for months. The pleasure associated with buying it is palpable. Now picture yourself taking that money and putting it into a savings account instead. It doesn't look so pleasurable, does it? In a Spending Mindset, it's almost impossible to imagine that saving money can be as fun as spending it on something desirable.

In summary, people generally tend to choose spending over saving for two very good reasons: Saving isn't fun and it feels like deprivation and spending money is fun and feels like an appropriate reward. Chapter 11 will wrestle the need for immediate gratification and provide alternative ways to view saving money that make it a significantly more attractive option.

Spending Mindset #5: Saving = Feeling Restricted and Deprived of "Things"

Key Takeaways

- In a Spending Mindset, spending money is seen as fun and desirable while saving money feels like self-sacrifice and deprivation.
- Saving money does not satisfy human beings' desire for immediate gratification and therefore decreases the drive for saving.
- Couples are far more compelled to spend money than save money – it's more fun in the moment and feels like a deserved reward.

CHAPTER 6

Spending Mindset #6: Saving = Spending Less on the Same Stuff

- *Spending Less Is Not Saving*
- *Couponing, Discounts, and Sales*
- *Key Takeaways*

Spending Less Is Not Saving

The key characteristic of Spending Mindset #6 is the tendency to believe that buying "smart" (i.e., buying on sale or getting a really good deal) automatically equates to saving money. Said another way, people believe that saving money and buying smart are the same thing. It sounds like this: "I saved $10.00 today because the store was having a sale" or "I got these clothes on sale today and saved a bunch of money." But is that really *saving* money? What if the purchased item wasn't really needed? What if the sale going on at the store encourages you to spend more than what you planned so you can take advantage of the great deals?

In the context of this book, buying smart is *not* by default the same thing as saving money. Saving money and buying smart are the same thing if—and only if—two conditions are met:

1. The item purchased that was on sale was an item that fulfilled a need.

2. The money not spent by buying smart will be put into a savings vehicle.

If these two conditions are met, then you truly did save $10.00 by buying on sale. The trick is that this is not usually the case and people get confused. They believe if they're buying smart, then they are in fact saving money. If the sale sticker on the clothes is what motivated a purchase (and not a need) and the "saved" $10.00 goes toward buying other sale items, that can hardly be considered saving money. Yet many people feel that even if the item purchased was not needed and the money not spent on the purchased item does not make its way to a bank account, it is still somehow "saved" money.

This false sense of saving money by getting a "good buy" makes people feel good about making purchases even if they didn't need the item in question in the first place. And when something feels good, you do it more often. Sales and bargains encourage increases in spending—and marketers know this. Marketers and retailers want people to equate buying their goods on sale as saving money. People feel better about buying when they're getting a good deal, and when people feel better about buying, they buy more. If you find a great deal on a new sweater, you buy two instead of one sometimes, don't you? Often, the money "left over" after getting a good deal gets spent on another good deal! Marketers and retailers do a great job of encouraging people to spend money unnecessarily while simultaneously giving them the feeling that they are saving money. The "buy two, get the third one free" ploy is a perfect example. This

Spending Mindset #6: Saving = Spending Less on the Same Stuff

"incredible deal" encourages you to buy more than what you really need (perhaps you don't even need it at all) in order to get a great deal on the third item (which you definitely don't need). How about scratch-and-save days? People tend to overspend in the hopes they will hit the jackpot—50 percent off their entire purchase. All of a sudden, you are "saving" money all over the place by buying things on sale and yet you have nothing left in your wallet when you get home and you have purchased things you don't really need.

In a Spending Mindset, people feel that buying smart equates to saving, when really it is only the illusion of saving money. Rather than saying, "I saved a bunch of money today!" what people should often be saying is, "I didn't spend as much money on these new clothes as I could have today!" Said that way, it really doesn't have the same ring to it and doesn't feel quite as good.

Couponing, Discounts, and Sales

Coupons, volume discounts, discount malls, online shopping, and buying on sale are all key components of good money management. They are excellent and appropriate behaviors for the savvy couple that is concerned with saving money and knows how to take advantage of these offers to maximize their savings when buying things they truly need. However, when couples are in a Spending Mindset, these practices tend to encourage unnecessary spending. This is why marketers invented these enticements in the first place. Marketers and retailers do not create enticements for buyers that will lose them money; they create "sales" and enticements because they know in the long run, people will end up spending more. Any ideas, practices, or enticements that are linked to "savings" but that actually encourage spending aren't really designed to encourage saving at all. Enticement tactics should never dictate whether or not you buy something, as tempting as it may be. The key to saving money is to build and practice the discipline to not spend on frivolous wants at all, no matter how good the deal looks. Part 2 will discuss how coupons and sales can be used effectively when buying things you need.

Key Takeaways

- In a Spending Mindset, the money that is "saved" by buying smart is spent on getting even more of the same things, which are wants rather than needs.
- Couples who get a "great deal" feel good about spending and can end up spending even more money to feel even better.
- Enticement tactics that encourage spending aren't really designed to encourage saving at all and should never dictate purchasing decisions.

CHAPTER 7

A Summary of the Spending Mindset

- *Does the Shoe Fit?*
- *The Path Forward*
- *Key Takeaways*

Does the Shoe Fit?

As a couple, do you recognize elements of yourselves as living in a Spending Mindset? Do you and your spouse tend to avoid intense money conversations because things invariably go badly when the topic is raised? Do you and your spouse keep your incomes separate and divide up household expenses? Did you find after doing the exercise in Chapter 3 that much of your money is being spent on wants masquerading as needs? Are you spending all the money you make and setting your budget at what you can afford? And how about the practice of saving money in your household? Is it a fun activity that holds the same pleasure and allure as spending money? Or do you find yourselves buying on sale, taking advantage of volume discounts and coupons to justify spending more money on items that are wanted but not needed? Very few couples live in a Spending Mindset all the time (although there are a few). However, it is likely that you and your partner exhibit some of these characteristics at least some of the time. These behaviors are not necessarily bad, but they are inconsistent with building wealth. Further, these patterns are very hard for couples to recognize. Rather than being only one way of thinking and behaving, they become unquestioned routines and habits. These beliefs become entrenched and accepted as "the way it is" rather than as mindsets or beliefs that can be changed. You can't change a mindset until you see it as one possible way to think rather than the *only* way to think.

If the Spending Mindsets explored here don't really describe you, what does? Is there a kind of thinking that is contributing to your inability to save money? Or, rather, your propensity to spend money unnecessarily? Spend some time to figure this out. It will be very hard to change your behavior until you see the thinking that's driving your current behaviors.

The Path Forward

In order to question routines and habits, you first need to recognize the thinking or paradigms in the background that are reinforcing those routines and habits. Part 1 exposed six of those paradigms, which you can now hopefully recognize in some your own thinking and behaviors. To create new routines and habits that are more consistent with building wealth, you need to create new paradigms. Part 2 introduces five new ways to think as a couple that are consistent with a Wealth Mindset. For some couples, these paradigms will be radically different from not only their past experience but from what they consider to be "normal" ways to think. Think about this: Being wealthy isn't normal either, but it's pretty nice! Try to explore with an open mind and resist the temptation to reject these paradigms outright. Very few couples will be living in a Wealth Mindset all the time (although there are a few), but those who spend more time there will be far more likely to save money and build a prosperous future.

Key Takeaways

- Spending Mindsets aren't necessarily "bad," but they are inconsistent with building wealth.
- To create new thinking that drives new behaviors, you first need to recognize the thinking or paradigms that are reinforcing current routines and habits.
- Wealth Mindsets represent new ways of thinking that can drive wealth-building behaviors.

PART 2

The Wealth Mindset

CHAPTER 8

Wealth Mindset #1: Deep Alignment on Financial Planning for the Future

- *Let's Talk Money*
- *Benefits of Money Talk*
- *Exercise: Creating Your Wealth Plan*
- *What If We Can't Agree?*
- *Key Takeaways*

Let's Talk Money

The foundational and perhaps most important characteristic of couples living in a Wealth Mindset is a deep alignment around household money matters. They have complete agreement on how their money will be spent and how their money will be saved. As many couples can attest, this is a significant accomplishment indeed. So how do couples get to this point in their relationship? Simply, they talk about money as frequently as they need to. Rather than being a topic that is avoided in the house, household finance is intentionally brought up as often as is necessary. Family spending, family saving and what the future looks like is talked about and talked about and talked about until the couple has complete alignment. In a Wealth Mindset, conversations about money are some of the most important conversations couples will ever have. Alignment is a tricky thing, though. It's not something that's every really "done." Couples can fall in and out of alignment from day to day. Couples need to manage and maintain their alignment over time. A couple can be completely aligned one day and drift out of alignment the next. Circumstances change, household priorities change and lifestyles change over time. Couples in a Wealth Mindset have to constantly manage their alignment to the savings plan they create. Alignment can only happen through dialogue. Couples who avoid talking about money will never be aligned on their short-term and long-term savings goals. Couples with kids who are old enough should take the time to explain these principles to their children and get them aligned to the family's savings plan as well. Not only will it help to give them an understanding of why their parents say "no" sometimes, but it might help them build a Wealth Mindset early in life as well.

Benefits of Money Talk

Ongoing and managed alignment around household finances has three significant benefits for couples. The first and most obvious is that creating and sticking to a savings plan will contribute to greater freedom and flexibility around both retirement goals and nearer-term goals such as paying off debts quickly or leaving a job to try a new venture or stay home with a new baby. Second, aligning to and sticking to a savings plan that builds a nest egg early on allows a couple to weather financial "storms" (such as the financial meltdown of 2008) or other unexpected significant expenses (such as major household or automotive repairs). Being prepared for these unforeseeable expenses alleviates much of the stress such events can cause, which leads to the third benefit of aligning around and sticking to a savings plan: increased stability in the relationship. This is true for any couple, but is especially so for young couples just starting out. The act of creating a plan together in and of itself is excellent for a relationship. The act of having difficult conversations and coming to agreement is a skill that will have numerous benefits for the couple as they navigate life's challenges together. The comfort and peace of mind that comes from financial security also contributes to marital stability. No one has to look too far to see the devastating impacts of the stresses on a couple that came from money problems. Marital stability is also bolstered by the fact that when couples have a short-term and long-term savings plan they have aligned around and follow, they fight less about money. In fact, when truly aligned, couples don't fight about money at all. Since we've been together, Erwin and I have had only one fight about how to spend our money. Not bad for more than twenty years and counting.

Exercise: Creating Your Wealth Plan

I've talked a lot about aligning around short-term and long-term savings goals. I can't tell you what your plans should be because they are unique to each couple. What matters is that you create one together, align on it, and take the actions necessary to fulfill it.

As a couple, map out your "wealth" plan. Focus on the tangible, material aspects of your wealth plan. Some questions you might want to answer include: How much money will we need to have so that one of us can stay home with a new baby? How much will we need to take that once-in-a-lifetime vacation or retire comfortably? What kind of lifestyle do we want to enjoy? Will we be spending our time on a beach after retirement or traveling around the world? How much money will we save every year to guarantee this future? Do something to make your goals tangible and real every day. For example, make a poster that symbolizes your goals and hang it up somewhere where you will see it every day. Or make a scrapbook and keep it somewhere handy so you can refer to it every day. When you're dealing with something that might seem far in the future or "out of reach," it is very important to make it tangible and real to keep the vision alive. Figure out a routine as a couple that will keep your wealth plan alive and fun.

What If We Can't Agree?

Perhaps you've tried to build a wealth plan together and it didn't get very far. One of you thought it was a good idea but the other thought it was useless. What if one partner wants to buy that sports car with the bonus check and the other wants to create an education savings plan for their preschooler? Alignment can take a long time and it can be a difficult path to navigate. Yet it is a road worth traveling no matter how difficult. Couples who do not align on savings goals are at financial risk, and financial risk can breed marital risk. It could put the marriage on an unstable foundation if alignment around one of the most important topics in the house is unattainable. Couples need to talk money early and often in the relationship to not only guarantee their financial future but to help solidify their marital future as well.

An important distinction can be made here between alignment and agreement. You may not agree on everything as a couple (in fact, it would be extremely odd if you could agree on everything), but you can still get aligned around your plan for saving money (including those areas that you don't agree on) and how you will handle those disagreements. For example, you may not agree with your spouse about the need to spend money on a new tennis racket and your spouse may not agree about your need to spend money on a weekend trip to New York. However, if you're aligned, you've decided that your financial goals allow for a certain amount of spending and that each of you has a certain allotment to spend in a way that works. Maybe the tennis racket gets the OK, but the weekend trip to New York gets trimmed by a night. Alignment allows couples to agree to disagree without compromising their financial goals.

Key Takeaways

- Couples living in a Wealth Mindset have deep alignment around household money matters.
- Alignment on household finances provides financial stability in the present and helps to set a course for a prosperous future.
- Couples who do the work to align around household finances are building a solid foundation for their marriage as well as their financial future.

CHAPTER 9

Wealth Mindset #2: Our Money, Our Future

- *Joining Finances*
- *Why Would We Join Finances?*
- *I Can't Give Up Control*
- *Exercise: Joining Your Finances Fully with Your Partner*
- *Key Takeaways*

Joining Finances

At this point in your journey of becoming a couple living in a Wealth Mindset, you should be speaking openly and honestly with each other about financial issues and having as many conversations as necessary to align (and maintain alignment) around your short- and long-term savings plans. The next milestone along the path to living in a Wealth Mindset is eliminating "my" money and "your" money and making those concepts things of the past. All household income becomes "our" money. That means a number of things, both tangible and intangible. On the intangible side, both spouses claim equal "credit" for the income coming into the house. One partner might earn significantly more than the other, but the assumption is that you are a team of equals. Not only does the couple relate to the income as joint, but all household expenses are owned by the couple as well. It logically follows then that when *all* income and expenses are jointly owned, buying decisions must be jointly owned as well. On the tangible side of the equation, bank accounts should become joint accounts into which all household income flows and all expenses are paid. Credit cards should be, for the most part, joint cards as well (at least the cards that are used for the majority of household expenditures).

Why Would We Join Finances?

Joining finances sounds simple enough, but what would compel a couple to do it, especially if things are working fine as they are? There are three possible benefits to consider:

1. It is far easier to manage savings plans (both short- and long-term) when you are using only one set of books, so to speak. Creating a unified spending and savings plan with two people managing their own accounts and finances is more complicated—and in a Wealth Mindset, we want to keep wealth building as simple as possible. Simplicity is important; it allows couples to save more money with less effort.

2. As discussed in Chapter 2, there are synergies that can be achieved by joining finances. Fewer accounts with higher balances typically mean fewer fees and higher interest-earning potential. Putting all of the expenses on a credit card that offers cash back makes more sense than keeping numerous credit cards with smaller balances that don't offer cash back incentives.

3. The third justification for joining finances is the stability it reinforces in the marriage. Even beyond the stability that gets created in aligning to a savings plan, there is something very powerful about joining your money in a relationship. It creates trust, commitment to each other and commitment to the future you are creating together. Once the wealth-minded couple has aligned on their savings plan, joining finances "seals" the deal.

I Can't Give Up Control

While joining finances makes good financial sense, it's easier said than done. The concept of completely joining finances is controversial for many people. A lot of people react strongly to the idea of giving up control of their money. People see possessing money as a determinant of independence and control and don't want to give either of those things up. Your willingness to share control really depends on how committed you are to realizing the future plan you have created together. If you have decided to live in a Wealth Mindset, have had heart-to-heart talks about money, and have aligned around a savings plan, then joining finances is the next step in making that plan become real. Rather than "giving up control," each of you is actually gaining control of newly combined finances and a new, prosperous future. Let's face it: Being financially independent provides the ultimate feeling of control.

If you don't fully trust your partner to join your finances, you are probably not aligned yet. That is not necessarily a bad thing; it just means you haven't fully dealt with all the issues you need to deal with. Keep talking. Figure out where the differences are and keep working it out until you both fully align and commit to your joint plan. At that point, the resistance to joining finances should subside. Having said that, if sharing finances is uncomfortable and you really cannot align on short- and long-term savings' goals, then the concepts outlined in this book may not work for you. Your marriage might present other challenges as well, but that is well beyond the scope of this book. One thing is certain: *If you don't trust your spouse enough to give him or her access to your income, then don't.* There is obvious risk in joining finances and if you don't feel comfortable doing so, then don't do it. If there is any risk that your partner will misappropriate your joint savings, then do not join finances.

Exercise: Joining Your Finances Fully with Your Partner

Envision joining your finances *fully* with your partner. Write down the top three to five reasons or concerns you have about doing so. Ask your partner to do the same. Plan a dinner or a night out and share your reasons with each other. Talk it out until you feel your concerns are clearly understood and you have both considered how they could be resolved. This may take a while, but it's extremely important and worth the effort.

Key Takeaways

- In a Wealth Mindset, couples think of all of the money coming into the household as "our money"; "my" money and "your" money are things of the past.
- Joining finances simplifies money management, provides

wealth-building synergies, enhances marital stability, and helps build wealth.
- If the couple is resistant to joining finances, they're probably not yet aligned on short-term and long-term savings plans and need to keep talking until they are aligned.

CHAPTER 10

Wealth Mindset #3: We Buy What We Need

- *What Couples in a Wealth Mindset Do Extremely Well*
- *Distinguishing Needs from Wants*
- *Exercise: Are You Sure You Need That?*
- *Prioritizing Your Spending Based on What You Need*
- *Distinguishing Real Needs from Automatic Purchases*
- *Exercise: Getting What You Need for Less Money*
- *Key Takeaways*

What Couples in a Wealth Mindset Do Extremely Well

Couples living in a Wealth Mindset do five things extremely well:

1. Distinguishing needs from wants (food is a need; designer shoes are a want).

2. Agreeing as a couple on what the needs and wants of the household are.

3. Prioritizing spending based on what is needed, not what can be afforded.

4. Separating real needs (food) from automatic purchasing

decisions (for example, food is a real need; buying that food from a restaurant is not).

5. Finding ways to fulfill needs in the most economical way possible (e.g., carpooling or buying a used Chevy rather than a new Lexus).

Distinguishing Needs from Wants

As already discussed in Chapter 3, wants and needs are two different things. But a clear distinction between the two is not always obvious and can depend on context. For example, designer shoes can be classified as a want in one context ("I want those shoes because everybody else has them") and a need in another context ("Designer shoes are an important part of the mandatory dress code at work"). One could argue that for many couples living in the United States, many if not most purchases could be considered wants because most basic survival needs (food, shelter) are satisfied. Therefore, living in a Wealth Mindset means constantly evaluating and reevaluating what is a need and what is a want as defined by the current household situation. Couples must agree on what the wants and needs in the relationship are. In some households, items that contribute to physical fitness (gym memberships, sports equipment, etc.) are considered needs because physical fitness is an important family value and purchases that contribute to the health and well-being of family members are needed, agreed-upon purchases. In other households, those purchases would be wants, and that's fine. What matters is that couples have clear rules and guidelines to distinguish wants from needs. These distinctions will be personal to each couple. Even within the couple itself, a gym membership could be a legitimate need for one person and a want for the other.

Exercise: Are You Sure You *Need* That?

- As a couple, align around the kind of purchasing decisions that will be classified as wants and those that will be needs. (Hint: If everything you buy feels like a need, you need to tighten up your definition of a need.)
- Bring out your table from Chapter 3 and reclassify your wants and needs as appropriate.
- Be sure to uncover wants masquerading as needs. (Hint: Starbucks coffee is not a need!)
- Now recalculate how much you spend on needs and how much you spend on wants.
- How much would you save if you stopped spending on wants?
- Begin to monitor your spending by reviewing your credit card bills, debit card statements, and all other bills and receipts on a monthly basis to ensure you are spending on what you as a couple have defined as needs.

Prioritizing Your Spending Based on What You Need

Once they have agreed on clear definitions and guidelines regarding wants and needs, couples in a Wealth Mindset use those rules to prioritize spending. Needs will be satisfied before wants, and many wants will not be satisfied at all depending on the couple's financial situation. It is important to note here that for couples in a Wealth Mindset, needs will drive buying decisions—not the amount of disposable income on hand or how much they can "afford." The amount of disposable income available should never determine what is needed and what is wanted. The criteria for distinguishing needs from wants should come from family values, health and well-being, and long-term financial goals. The wealth-minded couple that has all current needs satisfied doesn't change the criteria because they have an extra $1,000 in disposable income; rather, the $1,000 is put into savings.

Distinguishing Real Needs from Automatic Purchases

Wealth-minded couples are very adept at uncovering wants masquerading as needs. For example, they are very clear that buying lunch at a restaurant every day is a "want" in spite of the fact that food is a need. People want the convenience of buying lunch, and no doubt the delicious choices as well, but there are other, more economical options to satisfy this need. Some people bring a nice lunch from home almost every day (I do). The cost of this approach would be approximately $3.00/day. People who buy lunch out every day spend a minimum of between $7.00-$10.00/day, every day. The person who brings lunch from home saves approximately $5.00/day, which amounts to a total savings of around $1,150 after-tax dollars per year, based on 230 work days per year. Assuming the tax man takes 20 percent income tax per year, the average person would need to make $1,437.50 *and* work for 72 hours (based on a $20.00 per hour salary) to pay for those lunches out. That's a lot of hard work! Let's say both members of the couple stop buying lunches and begin to bring lunch from home each work day. Jointly, they would save $2,300 per year. Assuming they do so for thirty years and the money not spent on buying lunches out is invested in an account that earns them 5 percent per year, they will find themselves with $160,450 they would not otherwise have had. This is a significant amount of money. Even if the money saved made no interest, the couple would still be $69,000 ahead!

Wealth-minded couples are not only able to recognize wants masquerading as needs, but are also able to find economical ways to satisfy their needs in a positive way. I recently bought a fantastic new car. It's a Mazda 6 and I love it. It cost a little over $20,000 and I got 0 percent financing for five years. I needed a safe, economical and reliable commuter car that would get me to and from work each day. The Mazda 6 was exactly what I needed. I could have "afforded" a more expensive car, but I was able to satisfy this need in a very economical way. Figuring out how to satisfy your needs with the most economical solution is critical wealth-building skill.

Exercise: Getting What You Need for Less Money

For the next five purchases you make, write down exactly what it is you need before you make the purchase (and remember to make sure it really is a need, not a want).

- How much would you normally spend (or be willing to spend) to satisfy that need?
- For each need, think of at least three to five different alternatives to satisfy that need.
- Which option gives you the most benefits for the lowest price?

- Pick your best alternative that is less than the normal amount you would spend.
- How much below your normal amount can you go to satisfy your need? Make it a game!

Key Takeaways

- In a Wealth Mindset, couples agree on definitions of wants and needs in the household and periodically reevaluate if the definitions still apply or not.
- Couples that prioritize spending on needs rather than what they can afford spend less and save more.
- Finding the most economical ways to satisfy needs is a critical skill for building wealth.

CHAPTER 11

Wealth Mindset #4: Savings = Abundance and Freedom

- *Loosening the Grip of Immediate Gratification*
- *What Are You "Buying" by Saving?*
- *What Are You Gratifying by Spending?*
- *Exercise: Making Your Wealth Plan Alive and Visible*
- *How to Say "Yes" and Still Save Money*
- *Key Takeaways*

Loosening the Grip of Immediate Gratification

While the tendency of couples in a Spending Mindset is to see saving money as a form of self-sacrifice and deprivation, couples in a Wealth Mindset see saving as a ticket to abundance and freedom. They are able to challenge the need for immediate gratification—but how? How do they forego the joy and gratification of buying something that's winking at them, on sale in their favorite boutique, in favor of putting that money in the bank or in an investment for some future vision that seems so very far away? What can compel couples to forego immediate gratification?

Couples can develop their ability to forego the immediate gratification of spending money on that special something by giving at least equal weight (and preferably more weight) to a longer-term view and considering what they are "buying" by not spending the money now. Saving money only looks like a sacrifice when you don't have a clear picture of what you're "buying" instead. You have to convince your mind it's getting something in return for deferring immediate gratification.

What Are You "Buying" by Saving?

What couples are "buying" when they save is an appreciating asset: one piece of the long-term vision (that you hopefully created in the Chapter 8 Exercise "Creating your Wealth Plan") that gets closer to reality every day you stick to your plan. Depending on what you put in your plan, you might be buying peace of mind, early retirement, or a house at the beach. Whatever it is, it has to be specific, tangible and extremely desirable to you. Saving money only looks like a sacrifice when there is no clear picture of what you are buying instead. When you are clear that every time you put money into your saving account, you are "buying" a piece of your dream home, a percentage of a college education for your children, or the option to stay home to raise children, then it's more likely to stop feeling like a sacrifice. Rather, it starts to feel as if you are getting something extremely desirable, maybe even more desirable than the newest gadget tempting you. The key is to substitute what you're not buying right in front of you with something tangible and more desirable that you are buying instead. At the very minimum, with a clear vision of what you're buying, the need for immediate gratification will have less hold on you, enabling more savings than ever before. With our savings, Erwin and I were buying the freedom to leave either of our jobs at a moment's notice if we ever felt unhappy. We have built solid careers on never, ever feeling trapped in our jobs. We always knew that we could quit our jobs at any time without hurting our standard of living. That's been worth a *lot* to us over the years. When you're not trapped in your job, you have peace of mind that actually helps you perform better. For us, what we were buying by sticking to our savings plan was never something tangible. It was freedom, flexibility, independence, and peace of mind.

What Are You Gratifying by Spending?

Creating a more desirable picture of what you're buying instead of the latest gadget can be especially tricky for people who are not exactly sure what wants they are gratifying by spending. Are you buying the latest smartphone because you really need the latest functionality—or because it feels good to show your friends and colleagues that you have the latest technology? Is looking "cool" and innovative very important to you? You need to be honest with yourself here. Are you looking at buying a Lexus SUV instead of a minivan because you "won't be caught dead in a minivan" even though a minivan will satisfy your requirements and cost less than half the price of most luxury SUVs on the market? The more you can uncover about what's really motivating your purchases, the less grip that motivation will have on you and the easier it will be to paint a more desirable picture of what you're buying by saving the money instead. It's not a bad thing to want to appear innovative and cool to your friends and colleagues or to seem successful and well-off to your neighbors, but those pursuits can be costly. In the end, you have to ask yourself if that is more important to you than reaching your savings goals and all the benefits that could bring.

Exercise: Making your Wealth Plan Alive and Visible

Revisit your wealth plan from Chapter 8. If you haven't already, add to it the intangible aspects of your vision. What kind of freedom would achieving your plan give you? What feelings do you have? How much better will you sleep at night? Make a list of all the intangible things you would be "buying" by saving a dollar rather than spending a dollar. Find pictures to illustrate these intangible things and add them to your wealth plan "poster" or scrapbook. The more real you can make it for yourself, the easier it will be to forego the immediate gratification of buying what you want now.

How to Say "Yes" and Still Save Money

So far, this chapter has focused on bringing clarity and concreteness to the things you are "buying" by saying no to purchasing tangible things. Achieving this state of mind will help you avoid feeling deprived. While this is a very important skill to develop, you should also develop the ability to satisfy the need for immediate gratification in ways that cost significantly less money and therefore align to your short- and long-term savings strategy. After all, living in a Wealth Mindset can't always be about saying "no" to yourself, and there will be times when it makes sense to satisfy a want in the short term. Rather than

Wealth Mindset #4: Savings = Abundance and Freedom

saying "no," the game to be played is more of a "yes, but not like this." If you can find creative ways to get what you want that don't cost as much money, then there's little or no sacrifice at all.

Example 1: You're a coffee person and every workday morning (assume 230 work days per year), Monday through Friday, you buy a $4.00 latte. If you cut this practice out entirely, you would save $920.00 per year. Maybe you decide to start drinking water instead and you start jogging to give you the energy you need that caffeine is currently supplying. While that is a good strategy for saving money, it doesn't do much to satisfy your want for your morning latte. So let's say you buy a coffee machine ($30.00) and put it in your lunch room at work (if it doesn't have one). You also buy your milk frother ($25.00), your milk, and your coffee and make a latte yourself every morning. Conservatively, depending on the kind of coffee you buy, the cost per cup of supplies (coffee, milk, sugar, cups) is no more than $0.50. You save $3.50 every work day. Your coffee machine and frother will be paid for in 16 days ($55.00/$3.50 = 16). After those 16 days, when your fixed costs are paid for, you will be saving $805 per year just by making your own lattes. That seems like a really good compromise to me. You still get your morning latte and you save a lot of money over the course of the year. You could even take it one step further and organize a latte club at work, getting everyone to pitch in for the cost of your coffee machine and frother. That's a creative way of saying "yes, but not like this." In thirty years, if that savings were put into an account that earns 5 percent per year, it would grow to $56,157. For a couple, that could mean $112,000 just for making your own lattes during your careers.

Example 2: Erwin and I were paying around $132.00 per month for cable and Internet. We realized that we weren't watching enough television to justify the monthly cable charge, which accounted for about $60.00 of the monthly bill. Dropping cable altogether could have saved us $720.00 per year, but we enjoy the occasional movie. So we dropped cable and added Netflix instead at a monthly charge of $8.57. We're still enjoying the entertainment that we want but we're saving $50.00 per month, for a total of $600.00 of after-tax money per year. This is another example of saying "yes, but not like this," satisfying the need for gratification but also contributing to saving money. Saving money doesn't necessarily mean giving up the things you love the most. But it might mean changing the way you get those things, negotiating for a better deal, or finding an alternative to satisfy the need.

Key Takeaways

- Couples in a Wealth Mindset don't experience saving money as a sacrifice, nor do they feel deprived when deferring immediate gratification.
- Wealth-minded couples decide on and visualize tangible and intangible things they are "buying" by not spending money on the things that seem likely to provide more immediate gratification.
- Wealth-minded couples learn to apply the art of "yes, but not like this" to get what they want while spending significantly less money to get it.

CHAPTER 12

Wealth Mindset #5: Saving = *Not* Spending

- *The Art of Not Spending Money*
- *How to Use Deals and Discounts*
- *Key Takeaways*

The Art of *Not* Spending Money

For couples living in a Wealth Mindset, the prioritized list of needs is the criteria that determine whether to spend the household's disposable income (unless or until your savings plan targets are being met—more on this in Part 3). Money available for spending in combination with the prioritized needs is *the* trigger to go ahead and buy something. If an item is not needed, the money does not get spent even if the funds are available and the buy would be a really good deal. (An exception to this would be items that could serve as excellent investments or *occasionally* an item that would satisfy immediate gratification that can be purchased in a highly economic fashion after playing the "Yes, but not like this" game.) For many couples living in a Spending Mindset, the only condition necessary to spend money is whether the cash or credit is available. In a Spending

Mindset, *wants* in combination with available money (or credit) often drive the buying decisions. In a Wealth Mindset, *needs* in combination with available money drive the buying decisions. This is an important distinction. Couples in a Wealth Mindset have learned how *not* to spend money, no matter how good the deal looks, how badly they want it, or how much money they have available to spend. The pathway to saving money is to stop spending money when it doesn't need to be spent—a simple concept that is put in practice all too rarely. As discussed in detail in Chapter 6, buying smart does not necessarily equate to saving money, but it allows for the illusion of saving money. Couples need to stop fooling themselves by seeing buying smarter as the same thing as saving money. Having said that, buying smart *is* a critical wealth-building tool if it's done properly and in the right context; namely, the purchase has been jointly identified as a needed purchase and fits into the short- and long-term savings plans.

How to Use Deals and Discounts

Deals and discounts should never drive the decision to buy an item. Rather, they should trigger a purchase only when the item on sale has been identified by the couple as a prioritized need and the money is available to spend. Evaluating deals and discounts should trigger thoughts about *how* to buy an item, from whom, and when only after the item has been designated as a need. This is the context in which wealth-minded couples use deals, discounts, and sales. Deals and discounts can and should be used only to satisfy a need. Couples in a Wealth Mindset are very savvy about looking out for the best deals, using Internet sites that reveal the best prices, and negotiating and shopping during store discount days. Remember, stores use deals and discounts to encourage people to buy things they may not really need. Wealth-minded couples only allow deals and discounts to trigger their purchasing decisions when they have already decided that an item is needed and there is available money to purchase it.

Key Takeaways

- Wealth-minded couples view saving as the act of not spending money if there is no need to spend it, regardless of how good the deal looks, how badly they want the item in question, or how much they can afford.
- In a Wealth Mindset, the prioritized list of needs aligned to the savings plan triggers buying decisions.
- Deals, discounts, and sales should determine how, from whom, and when to buy items identified as "needed" for the household and not whether to buy an item.

CHAPTER 13

A Summary of the Wealth Mindset

- *Does the Shoe Fit?*
- *The Path Forward*
- *Key Takeaways*

Does the Shoe Fit?

As a couple, how often are you living in a Wealth Mindset? Are you deeply aligned on the financial future you are creating together? Have you talked and talked and talked to each other about your household finances to get to the point where you have joined your finances and consider all money and expenditures in the house as "joint"? Do you spend money only on what you both have decided are needs for the family and do you spend money on wants only after your savings goals have been met? Do you routinely find the most economical ways to satisfy your needs? Has saving money become a fun game for you to play together as a couple? Is saving money something that brings you joy and fun rather than feelings of deprivation? Finally, has it become clear to you that saving money is about not spending money, no matter how good the deal looks? If you answered "yes" to many of these questions, you are living in a Wealth

Mindset. Very few couples will be living in a Wealth Mindset all the time (although there are a few), but if you see yourself exhibiting most of these characteristics at least some of the time, you are laying a foundation for future prosperity. Having said that, even if you understand that thinking in these ways is more consistent with building wealth, the principles outlined in this book require discipline to put into practice. Almost everything around us is designed to keep people in a Spending Mindset, making it very easy for old ways of thinking and temptations to move in and reignite old behaviors.

The Path Forward

Couples need a plan to force new thinking and new behaviors and a way to reinforce and maintain them to prevent slipping back to the old Spending Mindsets. In my former career as an executive coach, I found that the best way for executives to form new thinking patterns and new behaviors was to commit to objectives that were only achievable if they were behaving in the new way. The status quo (their current thinking patterns and behaviors) was only going to get them more of the same. In other words, they would "box themselves in" by committing to a highly desirable goal that they knew couldn't be attained unless they thought and behaved differently. The determination to achieve this goal would force new ways of thinking and acting, enabling the goal to be achieved over time. As a couple, you first have to decide whether building your wealth is a highly desirable goal, and, most important, that you're willing to change how you think and act to achieve that goal. If you are currently living in a Wealth Mindset and know that your commitment to wealth is achievable, then congratulations! If, however, you are highly committed to wealth but find yourselves unable to get out of the Spending Mindsets, you need a strategy to "box yourself in." Part 3 of this book, the "Spend One, Save One Couple's Strategy for Wealth," is one way to do just that. It will help you box yourselves in until living in a Wealth Mindset becomes a habit rather than an exception. If you follow the suggestions explained in Part 3 and stay true and committed to your goal of achieving wealth, you will adopt new thinking and new behaviors around spending and saving.

Key Takeaways

- Wealth Mindsets are consistent with spending less money and saving more.
- Almost everything around us is designed to keep people in Spending Mindsets, making it very easy for old ways of thinking and temptations to move in and reignite old behaviors.
- Couples need a plan to force new thinking and new behaviors and a way to reinforce and maintain them to prevent slipping back into the old Spending Mindsets.

PART 3

The Spend One, Save One Couple's Strategy for Wealth: Bringing It All Together

CHAPTER 14

The Spend One, Save One Couple's Strategy for Wealth

- *Introduction*
- *What Is the Spend One, Save One Couple's Strategy for Wealth?*
- *Why Bother?*
- *Key Takeaways*

Introduction

To force new thinking and new behaviors, a couple needs to commit to a strategy that will "box them in" to a new approach and provide very little wiggle room to go back to old behaviors. This is similar to when people need to lose a lot of weight due to health reasons; rather than commit to losing a pound a week, they commit to doing a triathlon or something equally outrageous by their own standards. That commitment may seem completely ridiculous and unattainable when it's made, but a true determination to make it happen forces radical new ways of exercising, eating, and thinking about health and well-being. Similarly, a true commitment to the Spend One, Save One Couple's Strategy for Wealth can drive and reinforce new ways of thinking and behaving around spending and saving money in the household. It's now time to put new thinking and theory into practice and start building wealth!

What Is the Spend One, Save One Couple's Strategy for Wealth?

The Spend One, Save One Couple's Strategy for Wealth is pretty much what it sounds like. You and your partner are going to choose one income to spend and one income to save. I recommend saving the lower income and spending the higher income. Your mission is to carve out a lifestyle that works well for you and the family living solely on the higher income, aka the "spend income." The money left over from your spend income after you've covered all your living expenses (rent, utilities, debt, food necessities, etc.) is called "fun money." At the beginning, it might be very little (or none). No matter how little, you get to spend your fun money on whatever you decide to as a couple. It might be a weekly latte (if you're not already making your own), a lunch out, a new pair of shoes, or a weekend trip to New York City—whatever you want; it's up to you. The "save" income is automatically deposited into a savings account and redirected into appropriate savings vehicles, never to be touched.

So what are you thinking right now? Is this crazy? Are you thinking there is no way you could live on one income? That may be true, but it might also be true that you could. Or perhaps you are thinking that it sounds simple? In theory, the idea itself is very simple. It's not even a new concept. People talk about this strategy, but usually in response to some external event like getting ready for a maternity leave, for example, rather than employing it as a lifelong strategy. People have talked about it but very few couples are actually doing it. That's because the trick is in the execution. You have to be willing to do what it takes. So if you are thinking that living on one income will be easy, that's great. You just need to get started. If you think that living on one income would be impossible to execute, that's understandable; but be willing to suspend your disbelief and at least try it.

Why Bother?

For those of you who are skeptical about this strategy, ask yourself "Why would I bother trying this?" If this strategy sounds extreme, it's because it is. However, that's why the strategy can be effective. It's so extreme that it's going to force you to think differently about what you're spending money on. Most couples can't live on one income unless they come together, align on a plan, and radically alter their spending habits. So why would you bother doing this? Obviously, if you commit to the strategy, you are going to save more money than ever before. This will open up a lot of possibilities for future wealth. The second, less obvious reason to give this a try is for the difference it could make in your relationship. Really getting aligned and working together on such an audacious goal could bring you closer together and keep you close for years to come. Challenges like this can be really fun, especially when you're in it together. Given the possibility of wealth and a better marriage, I would ask why *not* bother?

Key Takeaways

- You are going to carve out a lifestyle spending only one of your incomes (the higher one).

- The "fun" money left over after paying expenses from the higher income can be spent on anything you want—the more indulgent the better!
- Committing to the strategy will force new behaviors and open up the possibility of wealth and a better marriage.

CHAPTER 15

Simplifying Your Money Management

- *Making Money Management Easy*
- *Making Lists: Savings Accounts and Debts*
- *Revisiting Your Need vs. Want Spending Habits*
- *Key Takeaways*

Making Money Management Easy

One of the most important aspects of building savings and reducing spending is reducing the number of accounts you are managing. There are three important reasons for this:

1. When you consolidate the number of accounts you have, you will be able to take advantage of better interest and/or lower service fees.

2. When you simplify your money management by having fewer accounts to follow, you will spend less time and effort managing them, which frees up time and energy to do other things.

3. The simpler your savings and debt portfolios are, the easier it will be to get 100 percent visibility into where

your money is going and how much money you are accumulating.

Because this is so important, the first task for you to take on in the Spend One, Save One Strategy is to detail your current bank accounts, credit cards, and loans.

Making Lists: Savings Accounts and Debts

You need to get a clear picture of what savings ("liquid assets") you have, such as savings accounts, checking accounts, CDs, etc., and what debts you have such as credit card balances, car loans, etc. As a couple, list in detail all the accounts with money in them and all the accounts you have that require payments. Be sure to include accounts outside of your bank or credit union. You're creating a roadmap to get to a future place, so it's critical to have an accurate picture of exactly where you are today. You want to accurately list every single entity and/or person that you currently owe money to and all of your accounts that have savings in them. It's important that neither one of you hides anything. You're aligning on your financial future and you need to align around how you're going to get there. Without an accurate picture of your current situation, that's going to be difficult. If you still feel the need to hide things from each other, then you are not aligned yet and you need to keep talking until you get there.

The table below suggests the details you'll want to list regarding all of your accounts (you will use this information in Chapter 16). This book is about saving money, so we're focused on liquid assets (excluding 401K, investment accounts, etc.) and the debts that directly impact your savings balance. When you feel more comfortable managing your finances, you may at some point want to build a more thorough financial picture that includes all of your assets including tax sheltered savings plans; however, for now, focus on cash in hand and cash going into other peoples' hands.

Example:

Name of Account	Name of Institution	Interest Rate	Amount	Fees?	Online Management Possible?	Utilizing Online Management?
Bank Accounts						
Savings Account	Bank B	0.25%	$310.25	$1.50 per debit	Yes	No
Checking Account	Bank A	0.05%	$230.90	$.75 per debit	Yes	Yes (online statements)
Loans & Mortgage(s)						
Furniture Loan	Furniture Retailer A	3%	$780.05	Late payment fees	No	No
Car Loan	Bank B	2.5%	$7,340.00	Late payment fees	Yes	Yes (automatic payment from Bank A)
Mortgage	Bank A	3.85%	$282,000	Late payment fees	Yes	Yes (automatic payment from Bank A)
Credit Cards						
Credit Card	Bank A	18%	$478.05	Late payment fees	Yes	No (statement mailed monthly; check written)
Credit Card	Clothes Retailer B	16%	$1,650.43	Late payment fees	Yes	No (statement mailed monthly; check written)

Be accurate. Locate the most current statements for each account and make sure you've got your facts straight. You may think your credit card interest rate is 18 percent, but it might turn out that you missed the most recent letter from your credit card company alerting you that the rate is actually now 21 percent. Dig around and make sure you have all your facts straight. Include accounts, cards, etc., that have no balance. If at any time you could use them to save or spend, you want to have it on your list.

Notice which savings accounts are paying more favorable interest rates. Spend whatever time you need to make your lists—the more detailed the better. Do this together. Some couples will get through this very quickly; for others, it might be a challenge.

If you're finding it difficult to make this list, note why this is. Which accounts are "easy" for you to track and manage because you can execute your transactions online? Online tracking and management is a key piece of making the Spend One, Save One Couple's Strategy for Wealth work because it simplifies things for you and gives you 100 percent visibility into your spending and savings. Are your accounts accessible online but you haven't registered yet? Are you getting paper statements for things but can't find them in the house because you haven't set up a filing system for those statements?

In the next chapter, we're going to establish systems to get full visibility into your finances, simplify your transactions, and ensure you are organized. For now, just be clear about all accounts that show your savings and all accounts that represent money owed to others ("spent" money). Your paycheck likely automatically goes into a bank account, which is easy to manage. Note which accounts you find difficult to manage. Perhaps you have to mail in a monthly payment to a retailer after receiving your statement in the mail and it seems always to be received late, incurring you extra fees. Remember, make sure your list is exhaustive. Don't kid yourself that small amounts of money ($20.00/month) don't really matter. It *all* matters. Pennies turn into dollars, dollars into hundreds of dollars, and hundreds of dollars into wealth. You have to account for everything. Once you've got it all listed, notice how much you jointly have in savings. Are you noticing that one of you is clearly a more skillful saver? That's a good thing to notice because it will help you determine which of you should be the primary money manager in the house. Take time to study your inventory and see what patterns emerge. Does one of you have several credit cards while the other has one or two? Are you paying a monthly maintenance fee on a bank account that could be reduced if you pooled your savings to achieve a minimum monthly balance level? Spend a lot of time analyzing and understanding what your current savings and spending patterns look like. This education is not on school curriculums; at least, I never saw this ever throughout my entire school career, including MBA School. People study accounting, but personal money management is left for people to figure out for themselves. Take the time now to understand the basics. Look at what you have and how you are managing your household finances.

Revisiting Your Need vs. Want Spending Habits

This is also a good time to reevaluate the needs and wants you aligned around in earlier chapters. Be honest with yourselves: Are you carrying liabilities for things that you don't need? If you decide certain things are wants, ask yourselves if you can get rid of them or at least get what you want for a lot less money. For example, if you're carrying an expensive loan payment for a luxury car, ask yourselves if the dealer has a more economical option and wouldn't in any way penalize you for trading in your current automobile for a newer one with a more affordable payment. This is easier said than done, but you're not actually doing anything yet; you're evaluating what could possibly be done and what impact that would have on your spending and saving scenario. Keep an open mind and explore every possible avenue.

Key Takeaways

- As a couple, make detailed lists to get full visibility into your savings and spending situation including all accounts with your money and all accounts showing money you owe.
- Make notes about what patterns you can see emerging from your inventory.
- Revisit your wants vs. needs spending commitments and determine what "want" spending can be minimized or even eliminated.

CHAPTER 16

Simplifying Your Money Management: Finding Synergies

- *Consolidating Your Bank Accounts*
- *Consolidating Your Debts*
- *A Note about Online Banking and Automatic Payments*
- *A Note About Credit Cards*
- *What's Next?*
- *Key Takeaways*

So far, you've taken the time to detail your savings and debts and you've revisited your spending habits to determine what "want" spending could be eliminated or at least satisfied in a more economical fashion. Now it's time to find synergies and simplify your money management. This chapter is about *how* you manage your savings and debts to minimize complexity and costs.

Before you study your situation, let's look at a possible scenario for some couples:

The Couple's Strategy for Building Wealth

Partner 1:

Name	Name of Institution	Interest Rate	Amount	Fees?	Online Management Possible?	Utilizing Online Management?
Bank Accounts						
Personal Savings (with debit card)	Bank A	0.25%	$478.05	$.50/debit	Yes	No (mail statement in monthly)
Joint Personal Savings Account	Bank A	0.24%–3.5% (tiered interest rate)	$4,020.00	$1.00/debit	Yes	No (although paperless statements are available)
Personal Checking Account	Bank B	0.10%	$60.00	$.45/check	Yes	No (monthly Statement mailed)
Personal Savings (with debit card)	Bank B	0.30%	$150.00	$.55/debit	Yes	No (although paperless statements are available)
Loans & Mortgage(s)						
Furniture Loan	Furniture Retailer	3%	$780.05	Interest	No	No
Car Loan	Bank A	3.25%	$3,300.00	Interest	Yes	Auto payment from personal checking account
Credit Cards						
Personal Credit Card	Bank A	18%	$1386.00	Interest	Yes	Yes (online credit card statements)
Personal Credit Card	Clothing Retailer A	19%	$420.00	Interest	Don't know	No (monthly statement mailed)

Partner 2:

Name	Name of Institution	Interest Rate	Amount	Fees?	Online Management Possible?	Utilizing Online Management?
Bank Accounts						
Personal Savings (with debit card)	Bank C	0.25%	$628.00	$.40/ debit	Yes	No (statement mailed monthly)
Joint Personal Savings Account	Bank A	0.24 –3.5% (tiered interest rate)	$4,020.00	$1.00/ debit	Yes	No (however paperless statements are available)
Personal Checking Account	Bank C	0.10%	$286.00	$.25/ check	Yes	No (monthly statement mailed)
Loans & Mortgage(s)						
Car Loan	Bank B	3.25%	$2,800.00	Interest	Yes	Auto payment from personal checking account
Credit Cards						
Personal Credit Card	Bank C	18%	$859.24	Interest	Yes	Yes (online credit card statements)
Personal Credit Card	Clothing Retailer B	15%	$53.00	Interest + $35.00 late payment charge	Yes	No
Personal Credit Card	Clothing Retailer C	18%	$356.12	Interest + $25.00 late payment charge	No	No

What's not ideal with this situation?

1. Together our couple has five credit cards across five different institutions, six bank accounts across three different banks (each with its own debit card with fees), and three loans for a total of fourteen financial entities. This is complicated to manage!

2. Because it's complicated to manage, it's easy to let a payment fall through the cracks, incurring fees and interest.

3. Loans are being carried at a higher interest rate than what the savings are earning in interest.

4. Automatic payments/online banking are not being fully utilized; manual management takes more time and effort.

5. It's very difficult in this scenario to get quick and easy visibility as to how they stand *as a couple*.

6. This couple is not taking advantage of possible benefits available if they joined accounts; for example, they might earn a higher interest rate if they had all of their savings in the same account or might benefit from a lower interest rate on debts if they amalgamated their loans and credit cards.

Even if this couple has decided to join finances in principle, they are living separate financial lives *practically* speaking, which takes more time and energy to manage. It's easy to fall into this scenario. A lot of people have too many credit cards. You are at the register about to buy several hundred dollars in clothing and you're offered a 25 percent discount if you apply for the store's credit card. You go with the best rate for your car loan, and the customer service representative insists you open a checking account through which to make payments and offers you a special "because you have a loan with us" interest rate if you open up a savings account. Over a few years, it's easy to see how you can end up with multiple accounts across multiple institutions. While there may be benefits in each case for justifying all those accounts, it's generally inefficient, difficult to manage, and potentially costly.

Consolidating Your Bank Accounts

How might this fictitious couple's scenario be simplified and how might they take advantage of the synergies available if they join finances? Their overall goal should be to minimize the number of financial institutions they do business with, maximize savings interest, minimize fees, and maximize online banking efficiencies. Here's how this couple might think about their current financial portfolio:

Savings Accounts: Savings accounts often have tiered interest rates, which means the more money you have in one, the more interest you make. Therefore, it makes sense to look at which savings account is going to give this couple the highest interest rate the more money they put in it. If they pool their savings, they'll likely get a higher interest rate. Higher balances also often allow for reduced fees. As it is a savings account, they should avoid getting a debit card with it (or if they get one, they should cut it up). Savings accounts typically charge high fees for debits and, after all, savings accounts are designed to accumulate savings, not to spend money. Savings accounts will be for money going in only, as a rule.

A note of caution is worth repeating here. If you are moving money from a personal account (you are the only signing authority on the account) to a joint account in which you both have signing authority, then your spouse will have access to the entire balance. If you are not comfortable with this, then don't do it. As I've said before, if you don't fully trust your spouse, then this strategy is probably not the strategy for you, and that's fine. There will be other tactics you can learn that will help you save.

Checking Accounts: Just as savings accounts are designed for saving (money coming in), checking accounts are designed for money going out. Therefore, this couple should pick a checking account that has the lowest fees possible. Think of a checking account as a "flow-through account," meaning you'll put just enough in to pay your bills and expenses and the money won't be there long; therefore, the interest rate really doesn't matter because money will never be in there long enough to collect interest anyway. That's what a savings account is for. Our couple will want a debit card with this account so that you can track every (and I mean *every*) purchase and every debit that's made from the account. This account may be used to set up automatic payments as well. Ideally, the savings account and checking account will be at the same financial institution. They should pick the institution that will give them the best "package" between the two accounts (highest interest rate on savings, lowest transaction fees on the checking). Chances are (and they should negotiate for this) their financial institution will offer a no-fee checking account if they maintain a savings account with a certain balance.

Consolidating Your Debts

Credit Cards: Erwin and I have one credit card that we both use that gives us cash back on most purchases. This cash back (we call it "free money") is deposited into our savings account on a monthly basis. You can't really beat that. We have one additional credit card only because we need it to shop at a particular retailer (which, by the way, also gives us the same cash back on most purchases). Those are the only two credit cards we use, and if we could get away with having one card, we would. Our couple should figure out which credit card to keep and close the rest. It's far easier to track expenses with fewer cards (and only one checking account). Ideally, the same institution can offer a cash back credit card along with great savings and checking accounts. If this doesn't work out, the couple should make sure they set up an automatic debit from the checking account to pay off the credit card (with no fees). Mailing in any bill payments should be avoided, as it takes too much time and payments can be lost or delayed, incurring fees. When you have 95 percent of your joint financial transactions going through three accounts (one savings, one checking, and one credit card), it not only minimizes complexity and provides efficiencies, but it also gives you nearly 100 percent visibility into your spending and saving habits. You can't change what you're doing until you know what you're doing. When structured this way, our couple will easily be able to see how much money is coming in and from where, as well as how much money is going out and to where. One caveat to this approach is if you are trying to build up your credit score. There is a lot of great information out there about how to build your credit score and occasionally having more credit cards and personal credit cards rather than joint cards might be advisable. Keep this in mind and consult a professional lender if you're in this situation.

Loans: This couple should have a look at their entire debt scenario and see if there is a way of consolidating their debt with one institution at the lowest possible rate. This depends of course on whether they are currently paying interest on any of their credit card debt which, at 18+ percent, is an absolute "no no." Using credit cards to buy more than you can afford is one of the worst financial habits you can have. Erwin and I use credit cards to "float" money (meaning it gives us an extra month to pay for something so those funds can earn a little bit of interest in our savings account) and to provide us with "free" money from our cashback plan. If this couple is paying interest on any card, they should consider getting a low-limit line of credit from their main financial institution at a lower interest rate that will allow them to pay down all of their credit card debt. They should bring their debts to their banker and say "What can you do for me to bring my interest rate down?" Ask for help. The goal is to minimize the interest being paid so they can pay down the principle faster. One debt is easier to manage than several. Finally, when all the consolidation is done, it's important to ensure that all remaining loans are automatically set up to pay from the checking account.

A Note about Online Banking and Automatic Payments

I avoid going into a bank if I can help it. I manage everything online. Every monthly bill that I can pay online is set up to do so automatically (preferably charged to my credit card so I can get cash back on the bill payment if the service provider will allow that without charging me extra). I pay my monthly credit card bill via online banking. My paycheck is automatically deposited to my account. I even transfer money to my hairdresser's account as well as my babysitter's! Utilizing online banking for as many transactions as possible has two significant benefits. First, online payments take very little time and can be done from anywhere you want (home, work, the park). Second, it gives you 100 percent visibility into how much money is coming in, how much money is going out, to whom, as it's happening, on a daily basis. It minimizes end-of-month surprises. It's far more difficult to track expenditures when you're dealing in cash. When everything is online, you can see trends in your spending and manage it more closely.

Taking all of these possibilities into account, here's a potential scenario for this couple going forward:

1. One joint checking account with a debit card and low or no fees (because they have a savings account at the same institution).

2. One joint savings account that pays the highest tiered interest rates.

3. One joint credit card that offers cash back directly deposited into the savings account.

4. One consolidated loan (at least for credit cards) at a favorably negotiated rate. Obviously, if the new institution can't give them a better rate than what they're paying, they should keep that loan where it is.

5. An effort to start utilizing online management wherever possible.

New Joint Account Scenario:

Name	Name of Institution	Interest Rate	Amount	Fees?	Online Management Possible?	Utilizing Online Management?
Bank Accounts							
Joint Personal Savings Account	Bank A	0.24%–3.5% (tiered interest rate)	$5,276.05	$1.00/debit	Yes	Yes!
Joint Personal Checking Account	Bank A (new account)	0.10%	$346.00	$.45/check	Yes	Yes!
Loans & Mortgage(s)							
Joint Consolidated Loan	Bank A	5%	$3,074.39	Not if banking at Bank A	Yes	Yes!
Furniture Loan (partner 1)	Furniture Retailer	3%	$780.05	Interest	No	No
Car Loan (partner 1)	Bank A	3.25%	$3,300.00	Interest	Yes	Yes! Auto payment from personal checking account.
Car Loan (partner 2)	Bank B	3.25%	$2,800.00	Interest	Yes	Yes! Auto payment from personal checking account.
Credit Cards							
Personal Credit Card	Bank A	18%	0 consolidated	Interest	Yes	Yes! Online credit card statements.

By taking these bold steps, our couple will have reduced their fees and created a dramatically simplified joint financial picture. Imagine going from a total of fourteen financial entities (savings, checking, credit cards, and loans) to seven! That's a 50 percent reduction in complexity, which creates better visibility and understanding, which translates into reduced costs and better tracking of expenses.

While this book is not about providing financial advice, it is worth noting in the scenario above that the money in the savings account is earning less interest than what's being paid in loan interest. Unless that savings money is "money for a rainy day" money, then this couple could consider using some of the savings to pay down debts. These are the kinds of decisions a really good personal banker can help determine. There are many, many experts out there that have been trained to advise people in situations like these. Ultimately, it's your decision, and not all advisors are created equal. Talk to people, listen to people, and let the experts help you make decisions that make sense for you. Remember the goals are to join your finances (if and only if you fully trust your partner and feel comfortable knowing your partner will have full access to all of your joint accounts), simplify your transactions, automate your transactions, and maintain 100 percent visibility into your transactions.

A Note about Credit Cards

You can't save money if you spend more money than you earn. Saving money means spending less money than you earn. Credit cards therefore need to be viewed as a convenient and safe way to buy items designated as "needed" by you and your spouse. Credit cards, under normal circumstances, must never be used to spend money that you don't have. If you cannot discipline yourself in this regard, then you must not use your credit cards. Use debit cards instead, but first ensure your bank does *not* let you go into overdraft (that will defeat the purpose of using a debit card instead of a credit card; further, the fees for overdraft protection are often exorbitant). So, if you can't use your credit cards to purchase only those items in your budget, cut them up. You may develop more discipline as you go, but in the short term, get rid of them. If you are working to establish a good credit score, talk to a professional lender about how you can do this without using your credit cards. You might have to cut up the cards, but keep a bill payment tied to the account to keep it active. Seek some professional advice on this.

What's Next?

Pull out the savings and debt lists you've created. What can you apply to your scenario that we've discussed in regard to our fictitious couple? It's not easy, but remember, once you simplify things, your life will get a lot easier and it will be worth it. Which financial institution can give you the best overall package—good rates, low fees, a widely accepted credit card, and great online banking? Does one of you have an excellent relationship at a certain institution that will help get you better rates? Take this time to reflect and once again make sure you're really ready to join finances. This is a big step and you and your spouse have to fully trust one another. In the next chapter, you're going to begin the transition to your simplified financial picture so you can begin to enjoy the clarity, savings, and peace of mind that comes with it.

Key Takeaways

- Joining finances means consolidating savings accounts, checking accounts, credit cards, and debts wherever it makes sense to simplify complexity, maximize interest, and minimize bank fees.
- The fewer the accounts, the easier they are to manage and the easier it is to get 100 percent visibility into your spending and savings habits.
- Online banking and automatic payments should be utilized fully to save time and provide daily tracking.

CHAPTER 17

Implement Your Spend One, Save One Couple's Strategy for Wealth

- *Take That to the Bank! Amalgamating Accounts and Consolidating Debts*
- *Automate! Automate! Automate!*
- *Choose Your Spend Income and Your Save Income*
- *Spending Your Fun Money on Something Really Fun!*
- *Key Takeaways*

In Chapter 16, we walked through the process and shared tools for amalgamating debt with one financial institution, combining savings and checking accounts where appropriate to get a better return or reduce fees, and choosing a joint credit card for the household. Now it's time for you to go to the bank to open and close accounts, consolidate debt where appropriate, and set up online banking to automate your savings and provide 100 percent visibility into your spending habits.

Take That to the Bank! Amalgamating Accounts and Consolidating Debts

Make an appointment at the financial institution you've decided has the best overall package for you, including savings account, checking account, credit card, and maybe a line of credit that can consolidate your debt. If neither of you likes the institution you're currently doing business with, you can always choose a new institution. Do some research. While there are some good online financial institutions available, I prefer having the option of visiting a branch to see a personal banking representative that can help me on those rare occasions when I need one. Make sure that the institution you choose has excellent online banking (and mobile banking if that's your preference). You want to be able to do all of your banking from your office, your living room, and/or your phone.

Make an appointment with a personal banker who will take the time to truly take care of you and can advise you on how best to consolidate your accounts, especially your debt. Go together so you both understand the services being offered and the terms of the agreement. Be sure to bring all you'll need to move money from your old institution to your new one (your checkbook, for example). Drain your old accounts of savings and deposit them into your new account. If you're consolidating debt, have the customer service representative help you coordinate this. And remember to always *ask* for reduced fees and better rates. You won't get if you don't ask and you might get if you do. Tell the banker your plan is to grow your savings so they view you as a good potential long-term customer. Everyone is hungry for business out there, but salespeople won't volunteer better deals for you—you have to ask.

Automate! Automate! Automate!

Once you've dramatically reduced the amount of financial entities in your portfolio, automate everything possible. You want to sign up for paperless billing and automatic debits for every bill possible. Have as many automatic payments going toward your credit card as you can rather than your debit card. It's easier to dispute charges on your credit card and you might be earning points or cash back for those purchases. This assumes of course that you'll be paying your credit card balance off every month. If you can't pay your credit card balance off every month, you're overspending and you need to cut back. You also want to make sure you can pay your credit card with an easy, no-charge transfer from your checking account. Any money that must come out of a bank account should come out of the checking account only. The checking account is for money going out; your savings account is for money coming in that won't be spent.

Choose Your Spend Income and Your Save Income

If you haven't already done so, decide which of your incomes you are going to save. Once you do, set up your save income to go into your savings account—the account that you won't be touching. If this is not possible and it must go into a checking account first, set up an automatic transfer for that paycheck to go into the savings account at the same time it is deposited into your checking account. You want to "hide" the save income in the savings account that will never be touched. As that balance builds and builds, the incentive to keep playing the Spend One, Save One game gets higher and higher. Once you have a significant amount saved (>$500), you can start considering mutual funds and other investments to help that savings grow even faster. This is truly the fun part of playing the Spend One, Save One game—watching your balance grow from week to week and month to month. If you can stick to the plan, you will truly be amazed at how your savings can grow.

Spending Your Fun Money on Something Really Fun!

Recall that the money left over from your spend income after all expenses are paid is your fun money. There may not be any fun money in the early days. For a while, you might be figuring it all out and discovering what you can cut back on and what you really can't. Having said that, even before there is fun money, decide what you will spend it on so you have something to look forward to. This is the time you can spend money on your most frivolous wants! You might even decide to save up your fun money until there is enough to really treat yourselves. While the Spend One, Save One strategy is definitely focused on the future, you have to treat yourself in the present too.

Key Takeaways

- Put your plan into action and go to the bank together to simplify your finances.
- Choose your spend income (most likely the larger one) and your save income and make sure your save income goes directly into your savings account, not to be touched.
- Plan to spend your fun money on something really fun that will keep you motivated to keep living on one income.

CHAPTER 18

What If the Spend One, Save One Couple's Strategy for Wealth Can't Work for You?

- *Try It and See How It Goes*
- *What If We Fail?*
- *Modifying the Plan*
- *Start Something, and Start Today!*
- *Key Takeaways*

Try It and See How It Goes

For many couples, saving an entire income in the household will seem impossible. But that's the point. It should seem impossible—because when you commit to something impossible, it forces you to think in new ways and try different things. You need to get unorthodox to make it work. This strategy will force you to think and act in completely new ways by design. If you keep doing things the same way you've always done them, then your future will look very much like the past. This strategy is going to force you into a very different path and potentially a very different future.

I know a couple that committed to the strategy. The wife wanted to buy some new clothes. There wasn't any fun money to buy new clothes. Rather than dip into their "no-touch" savings, she sold some existing clothes to a retail re-seller and used that money to buy new clothes. She never would have done this without her commitment to the strategy. It would not have happened because the thought wouldn't even have crossed her mind.

The best way to alter the path you're on around savings is to commit to something that seems impossible. It seems uncomfortable to make such a bold commitment because you know the way you think and act today won't make you successful. You need to remember that's the whole point. Be willing to feel uncomfortable and let your commitment start forcing new ways to think and behave. Committing to something that seems impossible will force you to come up with new behaviors. Many people will shy away from the Spend One, Save One strategy before they start it because "it's impossible" and "why would I attempt something that's impossible?" I think I've just answered that question. You would attempt it to force the new thinking and behaviors that will help you build wealth.

You, as a couple, have to be all the way in. You have to be willing to fully commit yourselves to pulling this off while thinking it seems impossible at the same time. You don't really know if it's possible or not until you try it. It just might be possible, and you really won't know until you fully commit to it.

What If We Fail?

If you can't pull it off, so what? Think of what you will accomplish if you truly commit to the strategy:

1. You will have come together as a couple in a new way and solidified your commitment to each other and to your future together.

2. You will have joined your finances, simplified your finances, automated your finances, and achieved 100 percent visibility into how you're spending money as a couple.

3. You will most certainly be saving more money that you ever have as a couple before.

So isn't all that worth it? Those are the outcomes you can have at a minimum if you put your heart and soul into making this work.

Modifying the Plan

If you can't save 100 percent of the "save" income, figure out what you can save from that income. Is it 90 percent? 80 percent? Maybe it's 10 percent to start with. Whatever that number is, set up that money to be transferred into savings every pay period, no matter what. As long as a savings commitment is forcing you to think and act differently as a couple and you're saving money, then you're winning the game. You might find as you "build the muscle" that the $200 per month (automatically deposited to an account) becomes $300 per month and so on until eventually the whole income is being saved. Saving money is a skill that builds over time. Like any skill, the more you practice, the better you get. After twenty plus years of being committed to this very subject, Erwin and I are still learning new things.

Start Something, and Start Today!

The most important thing in this game is to just get started. Follow the steps in the book. If it doesn't work out for you, you can always forget about it. There's no penalty for trying. Just get started and do something!

Key Takeaways

- Committing to something that looks impossible will force you to think and act differently.
- Committing to something that looks impossible will feel uncomfortable, but do it anyway.
- If you need to, modify the plan, but make sure the goal is still a goal that forces new thinking and new behaviors.

Conclusion

In today's turbulent markets, there is one sure way to build wealth: save money by spending less money than what you make. While the concept is very easy to understand, many people falter in the execution. Most couples are living in a Spending Mindset most of the time, buying lots of "stuff" that they really don't need. People are spending what they make, and then some. If they can step back and adopt the thinking and actions of a Wealth Mindset, the same couples will have a much better chance at building wealth. No couple lives in a Wealth Mindset all the time or in a Spending Mindset all the time. Couples have characteristics of both. However, our natural inclination, bolstered by savvy marketers and incredibly exciting new products, creates a momentum toward spending. Let's face it: Saving money is not sexy and therefore couples need to consciously work at keeping their thinking and actions geared toward saving. The Spend One, Save One Couple's Strategy for Wealth is one possible avenue to force couples to think and behave differently. The key is to get committed to something and get started. The worst case scenario is that it doesn't work and you go back to what you were doing the way you were doing it before. At the very least, the conversations that happen over the course of the journey will bring you closer together as a couple. So you really can't lose.

Wealth has different meaning and importance for every couple because money is a means to an end. The amount of wealth you want to accumulate depends on your ultimate goals and the short-term sacrifices you're willing to make for those longer term goals. For Erwin and me, our goal has always been to generate flexibility and freedom in our lives. Keeping that end goal in mind has been crucial to the success of our plan. What is your end goal and how will wealth help you achieve it? It is your ultimate goal that determines what your wealth plan should be. I wish you good fortune.

About the Author

Laura Bell, MBA is a Change Management Consultant, supporting Fortune 500 companies prepare for and execute major change initiatives and breakthrough performance. She is also a wife, a mother of three, and an expert wealth-builder. Laura and her husband, Erwin, have been living by the Spend One, Save One Couple's Strategy for Wealth for over 20 years. This book combines both sides of her life to present breakthrough thinking skills to guide readers as they pursue the fine art of saving money and building wealth.